The Search, The Finding & The Awakening

Harshitha Virupakshaiah

BookLeaf Publishing

India | USA | UK

Presentation by *BookLeaf Publishing*

Web: www.bookleafpub.com

E-mail: info@bookleafpub.com

ISBN: 9789363313552

First edition 2024

To My Dearest Niece, Sanya,

This is for you—a reminder that love and kindness can prevail, even amidst the conditioning of the world. Choose your own path, no matter the difficulties or judgments you may face. Reject the conformity of others' expectations, and instead, trust in the magic of your own soul.

Live authentically, guided by the principle of "Do No Harm & Take No Crap." In doing so, you'll forge a life that reflects your true essence.

My journey has been profoundly shaped by the pages of books. From my childhood escapes into stories that offered a better world for better feelings, my love for literature has only deepened with time.

Always learning from both books and quotes. After all, what are they if they aren't the words of a writer's experience or knowledge?

I would like to quote a few that resonate with my soul below:

"Thinking is difficult, that's why most people judge."

Carl Jung

"Courage is not the absence of fear, but the decision to act in spite of it."

Nelson Mandela

'It is our choices, Harry, that show what we truly are, far more than our abilities.'

Albus Dumbledore (Harry Potter)

'Do not pity the dead, Harry. Pity the living, and, above all, those who live without love."

Albus Dumbledore (Harry Potter)

"But you know, happiness can be found even in the darkest of times, if one only remembers to turn on the light."

Albus Dumbledore (Harry Potter)

"Love is not always gentle. Sometimes it demands that we fight for what we believe in, even if it means placing ourselves in danger."

Paulo Coelho

ACKNOWLEDGEMENT

First, I want to express my deepest gratitude to my parents, Virupakshaiah and Shashikala, whose unwavering love and support have been the cornerstone of my journey. Even when my choices seem unconventional or hard to understand, you stand with me with open hearts and open minds. Your encouragement has inspired me to chase my dreams and believe in myself. Thank you for your sacrifices, your wisdom, and for always being there for me. This book is as much yours as it is mine.

Second, I want to express my heartfelt gratitude to my mentor and guru, Abhijit K. Das. From the moment we met at work, he provided me with a platform to be my true self and excel in my career. His invaluable guidance and mentorship have transformed me into a better person and a writer, evidently. Thank you for fuelling my fire and illuminating my path. Your belief in me has paved the way for my authenticity to shine through, and for that, I am forever grateful.

Third, to all the people I still have and I've fallen apart in this journey of life: each one of them

has taught me valuable lessons. They have
helped me learn what to accept and how not to
be in life. I wish everyone nothing but peace.

PREFACE

All of my poems represent my emotions at various periods of life, both past and current.

This began as a form of emotional processing through journaling. Then I used poetry and turned it into art. By dropping ink and making words of feelings appear in the light of life.

The poems depict struggles with oneself, love, hope, kindness, faith, inner strength, heartbreak, absolute carelessness, and humanity's greed.

The poems outline the fruits of perpetual self-work. The tremendous courage and bravery rooted in the heart, with a never-quit perspective that always seeks a silver lining in every situation of life.

They speak of unconditional love and, above all, the underlying urge of the inner child to defy the rules set by the world.

To embark on creating one's own universe of unconditional love and kindness.

As the saying goes, there are no accidents in life;
it is a series of pre-planned occurrences
orchestrated by the cosmos.

Love, Live, and Laugh.

Remember, you are always the love that you
seek.

The Time and Place

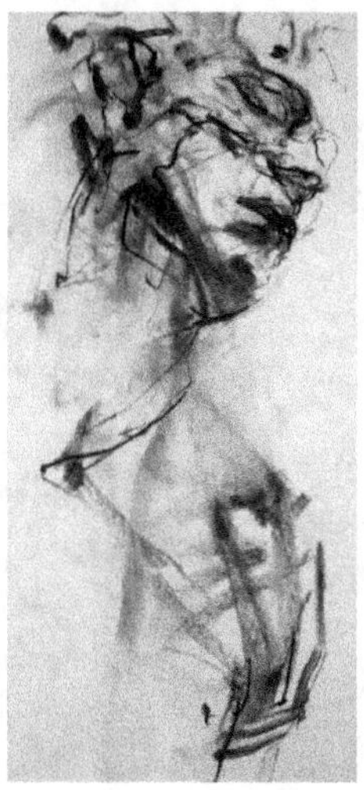

When do you know that the time is right?
When do you say what you want to say?
Do you do this when you think you know for
certain,
Or when you know it's in the uttermost
desperation that you're falling?
Or never at all?
Because they say to love and to have loved is
enough.
But is it enough to feel the care from a place that
isn't one's harbor?
What is the best fit for a person?
Why does there have to be a heart that needs an
outcome from this situation?

Amongst the dreams

Darling, you have to be in love with life.
And to be in love with life,
You must embed and embrace
Love for yourself the most.
It's all in the little things, you know?
Your smile, your laughter,
Even in your rugged irritations.
I have been dancing alone for a while, and
Now that you're here,
I want to see you breathe in this waltz of life,
Soaring among the dreams.

Your Smile

Dearest,

Edgar Poe agonizes about melancholic love.

I say the ravens are never untrue.

Love, my bloody heart—why do you get to love others so deeply?

That I could pour myself a cup of this love and be okay?

But what do we know about love and its mysterious ways?

I've always believed that love is the truest version of yourself.

I have laughed and cried with you in the depths of life.

Been present with all certainty.
And all that was needed was this forever and for
all my nows.
All I get to take away are the memories of your
smile.

The Unrequited

I want to strip you bare to the soul
And wrap you in love,
So deep that the oceans would tremble.
The sky would shiver with lightning,
All in the absence of light.
I am weary of breaking the patterns and my
heart,
Hoping to surrender, only to the waves,
To get an answer, to find peace within.
Why do I yearn for the only kind of love I have
known to give?
And, to be honest, why is this love of mine

So treacherously melancholic and always
unrequited?

Comfortability

I became comfortable with silence
When I realized that the shores of the mind
Cannot be tamed by the wants of life.
For I desired my want of love more than the
want of life.

I became comfortable with silence
When I started learning to love myself in
silence,
Away from the treacherous humanity,
Away from the ego.

I became comfortable with silence
When I realized that love is a game played,
Never won from others, but from oneself.

I became comfortable with silence when you
were gone.
Then, it was just life that had to be lived.
So I became comfortable with life too.

For a self who had put the soul in discomfort,
To always achieve a better self.
Walking away from you
Is a learning of kindness in comfort,
Only to realize the lack of protection
I had on the self.
A price I had to pay,
For the duality of comfortability.

Stardust

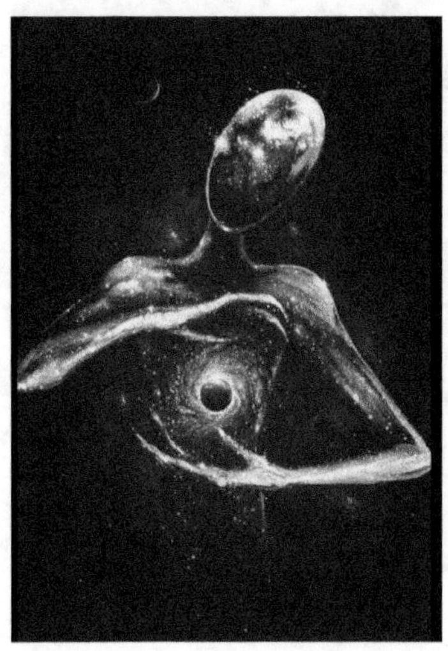

Twin flames, Soulmates, and Red-strings
All seem good when dreaming about,
But never in reality,
Unless you actually love yourself.
You see, a soul remains whole;
It cannot be divided,
And a merge can only occur between two
distinct splits of a whole.

So, yeah, I believed in all this, 'cause love
makes us mad.
Like Bukowski says, "Some lose all mind and
become soul, insane."
I went insane following and

Soulfully searching for love.
However, love can only be found, not searched.
See, everything happens because the universe
conspires for you,
Since, the universe and self are both made of the
same Stardust.

The Awakening

I am trying, amidst the empty shores,
Graciously among the illuminating moonshine.
Reaching in the dark for a calling to oneself is
what I'll serve.
For all I have known, having a soulless purpose
always feels like death's embrace.

I have dreaded the symphonies of this violin
During my darkest embers, because everything
in the universe conspired to make me be like
this.
Left with time and consciousness.

All this is to be for love, torn with an open heart
and soul,
Tragically awakening and scarring this heart and
soul once more.

Bones

The true cause of life is unaware.
Our love for callousness is never aware,
As it ebbs through the blood and generations.
How is it that, God, we are still surviving?
Living in loneliness and solitude,
But never for love.
The safe haven of oneself, along with a touch of
aloofness,
Is all that it needs to make one soulless.
This vicious humanity is always asking me to go
back and chill as bones within my earthly
mother's womb.

My Child of Heart

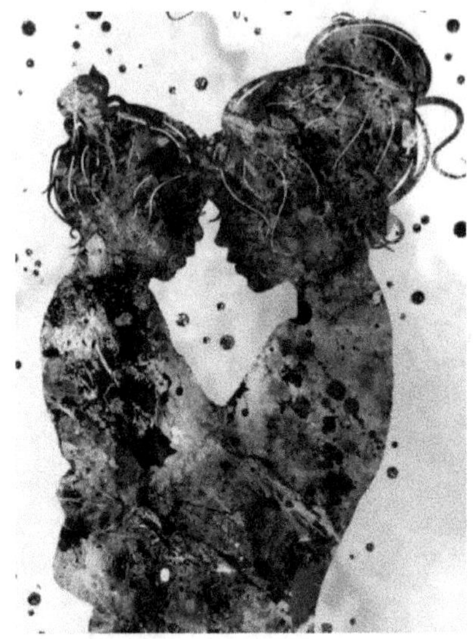

I can feel her melting within me,
My child of heart.
How long do I have with her?
That is not seen to be.
Fear not, for this is not something
Perishable like the wants of a human.

But it is of a self—the soul with which she is
merging.
For this is her fate—rebirth into a desire that can
never be.

Keeping her alive through art, devotion, and
service
Is and will always be the breath of life.

Like the way a sunflower follows her shine until
none remains,
She will go back to the waves,
Resting in the pool of eternal nostalgia,
Reminiscing about the paths she had to choose,
Leading to a witchfire born from the ashes of her
reverie.

The Way of Water

Why is it that we always wonder about the
people we love?
Having these intrepid thoughts,
Making me irrevocably believe in love at the
end.

All I need is the light shining in their eyes for
what I've done.
That's what's needed to face my devastating
separation,
And in darkness away from them.

For love and kindness, and for having
These two ingrained in my bones.
This is what I am forever grateful for my Mother
Earth,
Keeping me in the course of her water.

Sweetness of Life

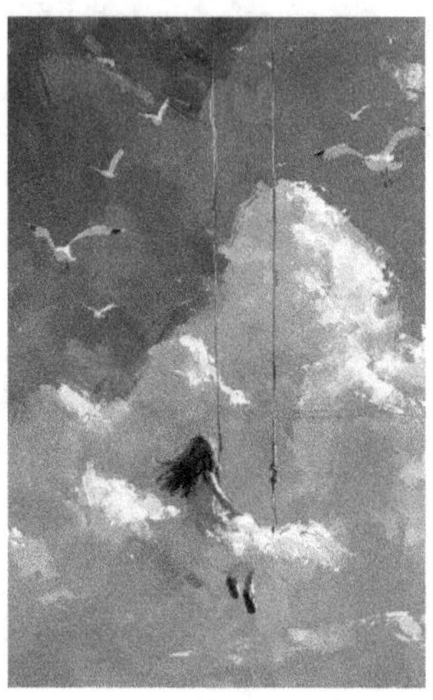

You are the universe in its entirety,
and the universe is you.

A powerful knowing and such a bittersweet
gesture of the universe to create you and I,
As the perennial twins in this vast nothingness.
For you and I, in this forever lonely path, evolve
or try to.

I am the universe, and the universe is me.
Isn't it lovely to see the zeal of creation.
Forever intertwined within our souls!

Now that I know this, and to be sharing the same stardust with another soul is gratifying enough. So, on this life's path, bathing in the essence of creation, is all I need to savor the sweetness of life.

Souls

Souls are eternally birthed by the universe.
As you see, the universe evolves; humanity tries to.
But what is lacking is compensated by meager cravings,
The choices ensure a fruitful change,
Whether one wants it or is ready for it.
For a soul's essence lies in its choices,
Taken either to evolve or to be afraid of its nature.
What do you believe?

Hope, Faith, Kindness, Love, and Peace can
either be labels
Or the essence of one's living,
Eternally artless and forever evolving.
For we are souls born from the universe.

Life's Kintsugi

I would like to go back,
Back to my days when I was a child,
When I greeted everything with wonder and
curiosity.
Pain and darkness have been my first friends.
I would like it to be so, for they have taught me
that the most enduring thing
Is to desire and to love oneself thoroughly.
For love takes all pain and turns it into life's
kintsugi,
Binding every choice made, shaping to create
one's reality.
For life is a game of 'Yes' and 'No.'

In the light of Life

Tell me about life, and I'll tell you about love.
Tell me about love, and I'll tell you about grace.
Tell me about grace, and I'll tell you about
kindness.
But don't converse with me about what's right;
Speak to me about what's being enjoyed at the
moment.
Don't talk about the woes; show the fire that
lights up life.
Tell me more about what perks the soul's light,
Buried deep within the heart.
Loving life is all I have been doing in different
ways.

But for now, let me pin this in the purest way
possible:
By dropping ink, words of feeling appear in the
light of life.

Oh, the Cities!

The cities, oh! The cities that make you see and
feel,
Bringing out the deepest desires
To the darkest interactions with oneself.

The cities, oh! The cities,
With those sparkly lights like neon signs of love,
Making you hula-hoop around your humanity.

The cities, oh! The cities, bright with
opportunities, housing all dreams within
realities,

Breezing through the trees of concrete life,
Showering those clouds of emotions.

Alas, the cities that ever neglect their
nature-nurture cycle of being,
Showing who you could be to what you are;
As what is dealt with is always deciphered by
one's choices taken.

The cities, oh! The cities, tantalizing forever;
Bathing in the limelight under the moon!

Change

When does change happen?
Is it when you're amidst your dreadful fears?
To break free from the demons in your mind?
Or is it when you shed a skin of yours in
relevance to a snake's shedding to protect
oneself?
Or will it be when you've seen, heard, and felt
enough of the woes?
Since the world has forgotten its purpose of
living in harmony.
However you take change, it happens.
All that is needed is to savor Mother Earth's
blessings as you change.

As I see it, change for myself is that the heart
shows the way and the mind sees it all,
While the soul embraces the path of
metamorphosis.

It is what it is.

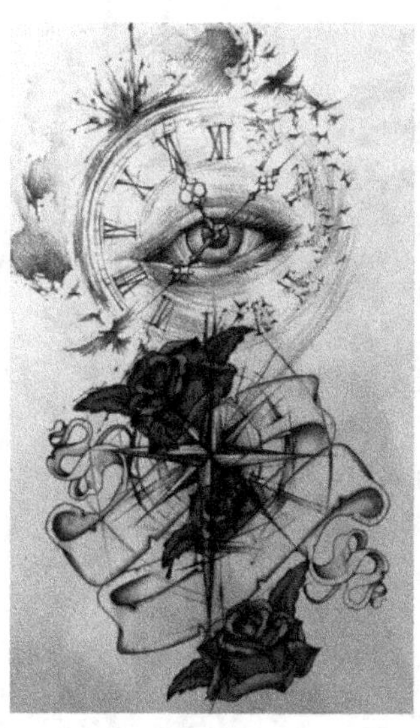

It is what it is.
Such a profound phrase of words,
Having no meaning of its own,
But entirely up to the reader's knowing:
To take what is given by time;
To show oneself what could be.
To breathe the courage of life to live;
To take arms against the storms of the mind;
To live with the soul's purpose;
To endure the realities created by the self.
It is what it is.
The power lies in the construct of being.
So, whatever will, shall be in the time of life.

Dancing with the Demons

Fighting is not my first choice,
But all I had to do was fight the world and its
conformity.
Ever since I was a child,
I have been taught how to be and how not to be.
Never was I told by many, but a few that
It is I who must show the world who I am
innately.
It is I who must decide the path or create it if it
does not yet exist.

As the world has forgotten its loving purpose of
evolution,
Stuck in the spiral of materialistic and shallow
choices of living,
Surviving one day to the next, never holding out
a hand to care for or to love another,
But living in the greed of the future, never for
now.
So, I choose dancing with my demons eternally,
As it reveals to me the reality of the self,
Always leading to the soul's divine purpose of
living.
A gracious gift from my Mother Earth.

Being Love

Darling, trust me, living life is easy
When you know the trick to it.
The trick is love.

They say love is in the air;
I never quite understood this until
This unconditional love of mine
Wrapped me up and protected me
In all the whirlwinds of uncertainty.

Rumi says "You have to keep breaking your
heart until it opens."

All I have done is from the naivety of my
childhood.
Until this certainty of adulthood
Is break my heart
By pouring love and trusting others,
Only for it to be broken by people who stay in
denial and fear,
And expecting them to love.

Until finally, I stand here, declaring to the world
That I am love and when you are love,
You don't expect anyone to give love to you.
Because you just become love,
The same way you become soul,
Always reflecting in the energy you walk by,
blessed by Mother Earth.

In the Rhythm of Dark & Light

The darkness paves way for the light.
The light shines on what is in the dark.
For how one uses what is shown
Is for the self to take action,
Depending on the flip of the thoughts.

Because when thoughts, emotions, and purpose
align,
Is when the alchemy of magic is born within
one's soul,
Always willing to dance with the eternal
witchfire created.

As Mother Earth has always shown the way,
In a way, the ashes blend with water.
In a way, the fire incinerates the living to ashes.
In a way, the earth brings life to being,
In a way, the air allows for a breath of life.
In a way, space creates all water, fire, earth, and
air.
For a magical soul is always immersed
In the rhythm of dark and light.

Oh, dear heart

Oh, dear heart, how beautiful you are,
Beating amidst the emotions of despair.
Utterly hopeless, faithless, and armless; you
beat.
A beauty of weakness, if taken to be,
For the love and kindness that you have for
others
Is never something that you have given to
yourself.

Oh, dear heart, how somber you are,

Throwing yourself at the scraps of affection
That always seem to be illusions.
Bleeding, withering, broken into countless
pieces,
Never to be woven again.
Walking through eternal fire seems
To be the calling that has been chosen.

Oh, dear heart, how lovely you are,
For something so sweet, encompassed by the
soul,
Only to be trodden on by the desires you have,
Breaking your mind, body, and soul again and
again,
Only to never gain the value you deserve,
always.

Oh, dear heart, how gaunt you are,
For all time has shown not to believe in others,
and still, you try.
Like a hopeless fool, wanting, desiring, waiting,
breathing for the same love you hold,
Handled carelessly by the clumsy hands of
humans.

Oh, dear heart, how weary you are,
Beating day by day with diminishing hope for
life.

No matter the creation of the mind, no matter the
abundance of knowing,
Still, like a babe, you yearn for love, an emotion
that is unattainable.

Do you not care for yourself?
Do you despair of the heart that you are?
Do you mourn the life bestowed by Mother
Earth?
How was this walk through fire,
Which seemed so easy then, so excruciating
now?
Do you not thirst for anything anymore?
For love seems to be your peril in life, a reverie
of a foolish child.

Oh, dear heart, I beg you to be,
To find a zeal to hold, to find a berth to breathe
the air of hope,
To love yourself unconditionally.
To weave all the shattered pieces through the
veins of blood,
To remove the veil of love, to stop tossing and
turning in the dark,
To ensnare the beauty of life, vividly present in
all life around you.
Now at the crossroads of ever being and letting
go,

Go fall into the abyss and bury the heart that you
are, if need be.
Be born again, like the phoenix you are meant to
be,
Singing the eternal haunting song of love.

Blend with Others

The pull of the warmth, wished for in childhood
Was ever that I longed for.
The safety net created out of the wisps of the lies
Was believed to be the utter truth; all an illusion
shown.
For I did think of the repercussions that
I would have my heart go through, but never like
this.
Thinking that my love would be strong enough
to salvage my heart in any situation.

Pity the girl I was, who didn't think of herself
ever.
Loathe the atrocities committed by time.
For neither can I want to blame anyone for what
happened, nor
The girl who was brave enough to follow her
feelings against fate.

For what followed wouldn't be anything new,
but it destroyed the girl I was.
I burned away my past self to emerge from the
ashes as the woman I needed to be for
myself.
For the men and so-called friends that I have
loved
Only know how to take and feed their egos with
the love given,
Never wanting to care about the impact of their
words and actions.

Used and depleted, here I stand.
Yet I try to build a life for the woman I am, for
the girl who had loved everything.
In the middle of creation, doubt and fear creep
in.
Lost and hopeless, losing faith in love.
It tires me to the bone, always thinking of the
end.

I crave relief, crying over a lost warmth that was never mine.
Proving for eternity that a lone wolf, after leaving her pack, should never try to blend in with others.
But to always believe she is enough to endure alone in her solitude,
For all eternity, against this wretched world.

Starseed

Settling in the dark,
Awaiting this abyss's lark,
Since despair seems to have taken root,
Holding me back from being afoot,
As my truth seems to have blended into
another's shadow,
Leading me into the devil's den, awaiting a
death blow.

Never have I been through this realm of
hopelessness,
Always bending down to the devil's demons in
absoluteness.
Craving relief from the intricacies of being
Is something of a reverie that has been reeling
Within this shattered heart.

Time for another adventure of love.
As it ever was in this forever rove.
All of this is obsolete; let me grab a bark,
Pull myself up, leaving the soul's lamenting
footmark
On Earth, to forever embark on my creation's
spark.

As this love of mine is nothing less than protean,
Piercing my soul with words of paean,
Molding the intricate forms of being into a foal,
Finally taking the Devil's reins.
To rise up from the dark veins
Into the life that can be.
For I am a starseed whipped from the foal to be
free.

Treasure of Abundance

Trusting the cords of letters,
Whispering of a magical tether.
Laying the foundation of values and virtues,
Of the self, always the knights in shining armor
to the rescue
From the dark ineptitude of a thought.
Wisps of love, hope, faith and kindness brought,
All from the imagination of a creator
Into the vacant soul for the greater.

Its knowledge in abundance,
Forever boundless, removing the self's
reluctance.
Only to birth the song of unity, of the mind and
heart,
With the soul to forever hold the incandescent
self's art.
Around the realms to see
The power of thee,
To build a life of knowing and to be eternally
free.
Such is the might of words, stringing along the
reader,
To mold a restless soul into a believer.
For the treasure of abundance is in books,
For a self to create a life of limitless routes.

I dream of a dream

I dream of a dream,
Of the reverencing humanity, steeped in the
essence of kindness.
Their ethos, seen in all realms for its rightness.
I know now that the above is not a dream but
another true perception.
Woefully, it is the avaricious trait of self,
adorned in possession,
Bringing all light to dark, shoving one
generation after another into obsession.

Of arrogance, of fancies in a fleeting semblance
of a true persona.

I was born of nothing, own nothing, and belong
to nothing.
Is that why I see so truly the desperation of the
beings suffering in cunning?
The blood, thorough and through, washes away
all sins as trivial.
Behold, the world in its state of heightened
greed.
No, not yet, for they are yet to kill hope, faith,
and authenticity like weeds.

I have traveled beneath the dark skies created by
the beings, again and again.
Having not stopped for respite, fighting in
futility to show the love that it needs to gain.
For once, I want to forget the world, which
makes my blood run cold
To attain penance and panacea for the sickness
of beings so capriciously bold.

Change is a wish that is set aside in this realm of
humanity.
Seamlessly moving from one being to another is
a facile demand of the current reality.
People toyed, and things wooed.

Oh, God, do you need more to turn it all into
ash? Is my wish so crude?
For all you have given us, a beaming soul of
creation!
Yet, the beings always move from one meager
thing to another for recreation!

Lost in the flow of time, never carving a better
world.
Perhaps there might be hope, as others like me
surely exist, curled.
Underneath all the darkness of humanity,
fighting in vain.
For the true state of this realm,
To bring about the birth of a kind world.
Only if that were possible; hence, I dream of a
dream
Of a kind world, a true perception swept away in
beings' selfish stream.

Beauty of Love

Love, from birth to ashes, a multitude of
passions,
Seen in the eye through the lashes.
Chosen time and again,
Either a wish or a bane.
What do I know of love
When I have just started to crawl in this rove?

I love my love an infinite number of times, in
infinite ways.
Sometimes in anger of whys,
Sometimes along the fanciful lies,
Aching in memories, to dancing in their graces.

I love my love, making me face the demon with
many faces,
Helping me learn about myself in all life's paces.
All through the dark and into the light,
A pattern from childhood surpassed in right.

It's said that love isn't a mere feeling but a
choice.
How is it that my choices keep pecking at my
soul's voice?
Irrationalizing the mind in a puddle,
Always leaving the heart's wishes in rubble.

I love my love, for it shows that wishes do come
true.
I try to pay no mind to all the flashes of blue,
A cycle of woes ending with me.
For the mother, father, and the love,
All have my love, even through strife.
So I try to love my love, for it's the beauty of the
given life.

Terror

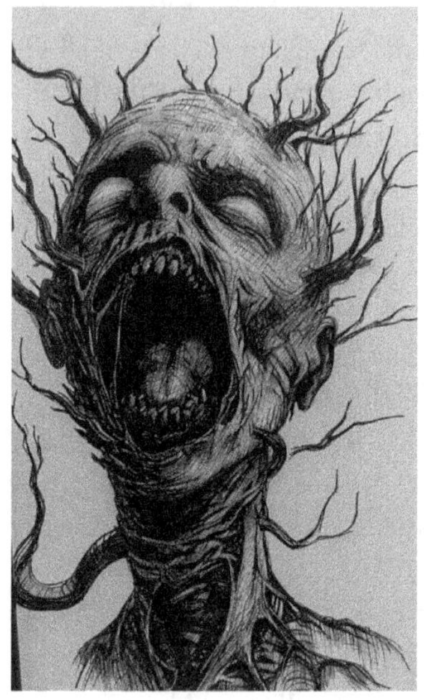

Do you know the feeling of terror?
The trembling of veins,
in your shoulder, hooked with reins;
crawling down through your spine.
Do you know what it lacks?
An irrevocable self-trust.

When your body thinks it's your reality
and everything is scary,
the dredge of overthinking is in a spiral,

questioning your reality, emotions are viral.
Manipulation is easy; that is a power one has
over another self.
by observing to entertain, take something for
mere fun.

Be careful; in this reality, self-trust is vital,
gained leaning into overthinking.
Sit there, for it's the fear of "what if,"
for the situations that are indictable.
No matter the choice taken, you do not bother;
safety is a secondary thing, found in another.

Those who are close are to make you feel safe,
especially when it is most unsafe.
And if they don't strain for safety,
making you insignificant,
take back the power by refusing to play
In situations, in their pitiful thinking.
There is no need to stay.

Terror in the mind ceases to exist, helping the
bearer
rise above the snarer.
For empathy is not a skill;
It is the might of your soul in its will.
something that people are born with.
It's not a learning; it's a state of being.

Dropping the reins from the shoulders,
away from the pitiful holders,
a beauty in the transition of self,
From invalidation to credence,
a self's allegiance,
changing Terror to be Indestructible.

In the end

A journey, ongoing,
eternally, through countless beings.
The cycle of never-ending expectations,
tirelessly running in a circle of anticipation,
only to judge and never to think,
all for something achievable.

Kindness, love, and laughter,
Partaken in patches; never alive
through all ways of life in this realm.

Such a simple thing: being kind.
Powerful to know all the things it took to be,
to make light of something that brings joy to all,
to offer solace through a thing called friendship,
to tell them that you are there,
right next to them.
To run into the wilderness.
To enjoy life, like notes of a song,
to be a shade when the other is in need.

A beauty of hearts,
to have found such a kind of solace in another
kind soul,
To make light of life when it's most difficult.
Such a precious thing is to be saved,
For at the end of the dark,
to have known another kind soul.
There is no more that anyone can take from this
realm.

Trust

The one that washes away the tingling,
Bearing hope out from within, all sprinkling.
An ally from within, merged from the dark into
the light.
Self-made, completely given into might.
Trusting the decanted descent,
All doubts bent,
Only to make one better.
An oath written in a letter.
Through the phases called Time,
An eternal ally or foe, if chosen out of a dime.

Scattered are the weaves of the past; nothing to
improve there.
The only question to be asked is where.
Of the light leading its way,
The embers of darkness discarded away.
A feeling of self-belief so powerful, yet an
enigma,
Of the clarity of now, mooring away the stigma.
Belief in a better way of the now;
Trust, a hard-earned belief, an antidote to all
phases,
Carving peace in all life's mazes.

North Star

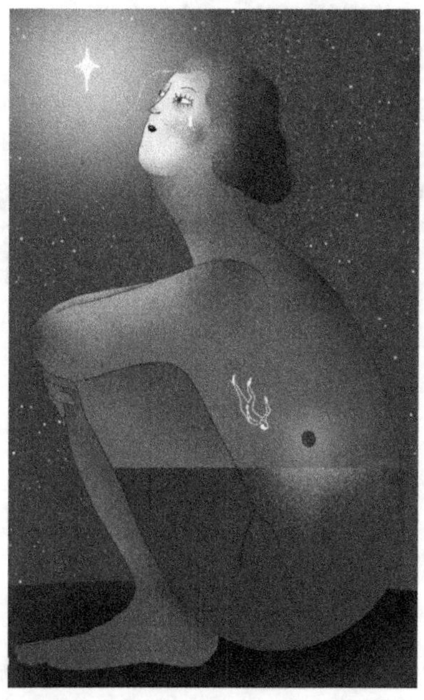

A hope of an illuminous beam,
Every speck forged from dark into a light
stream.
Ever shiny with its charm, enticing wide-eyed
beings,
Igniting dreams, sparks of magical tapestries
birthed in the mind.
Words spoken, deeds echoed-
Strings of life woven through the fabric of time,
Never pestering about the construct of a dime.

A way of living shown to the ancients,
Allowing it to be relayed through generational
claimants.
Forever showing a self of the marvelousness of
being.
Creation and love entwined in a soul far-seeing.
For a self to exceed its false expectations set
From a shallow world of inset greed, without a
fret.

For the way shown from within,
From the soul to the skin,
A replica of the illuminous beam.
Showing that the soul and the universe are
Both flowing from the same canvas.
A self's compass forever brings life to a par,
A North Star awoken from the self's slumber.

Bittersweet Tie

Rivers of blood,
Neither can wash away nor bury
The viciousness of a self awakened in a flood,
Throwing the facades of drawbacks
And battering the mind with guilt and shame
For when something is conditioned.
Deep-seated from childhood,
Until this adulthood showing
the unawareness, bearing a pattern
Ingrained as a trait of self.

Believe the heart; trust the feeling.
for it to show where to pour.
The essence of self, to break the cycle
Of paradigms, only to birth
The awareness of light and dark,
Forever showing the beauty of the
Bittersweet tie of pain and change
All from the love and kindness of a self.

Boundaries

Boundaries are vital
In a chosen life.
To keep a noble title,
Preparing oneself for a better now,
Forgetting the worries about how,
Laying in the foundation of a fallen self,
Only to rise from the ashes as an immaculate elf.

The experiences bring about feelings and
memories;
Choose to keep the ones that made the heart
chirpy,

For these are life's treasures
Of the love shown through self, again and again,
From the bottomless pit of kindness to reign,
Weaving in the before, now, and after
To make one's life more crafter.

A love so kind and powerful
To change the course of life in a windful
All it needs is a self, seering through
The ways of life, baking like a brew,
To take the knowing of the alchemy
Of turning dark to light, like a symphony.
An untamable force of a self in its move.

Moonbeams

A spellbinding, a trick of the eyes,
A large orb with littles dark patches.
The rationale of the gravity written in,
Shares the strange mind.

A dazzling eternal beauty of a circle,
Forever pridefully wearing the scars,
Always moving from nothing to glowing,
In a cycle for all eternity,
Tells the feathered heart.

Such a distinction in self,
A beauty of comparison is sought,
Of all thoughts to clouds,
The multitude of stars to beings,
The vast canvas of sky to the mind unexplored,
The story of the moonshine roars.

Evidently making a self realize
Of the vast nothingness of life
To make meaning in line with the heart and
mind,
Showing the soul its true purpose of living.
In all uncertainty, giving into the strength of
love,
Showing the wonders of life, an eternal dance of
Chaos and Order.

All in the shores of the mind,
Of a self in all timelessness,
While adoring the silent, calm thunder
of Moonbeams.

Shedding Trauma

Trauma, a word of the new world,
Never known to the creatures of the mute,
Only to the beings gifted with a voice unfurled.
A blind spot until the self awakens in fruit,
Conformed from the experiences one had,
From the babe through the lives of meaningless
gad.

The choices taken, unaware of the pattern,
To suffice the feeling of the now.
Either taken by the self or the other,
To gain power, restrain another.
The repercussions follow without a buffer,

Done by deeds void of thinking, kindness, and
love for others.

The self, which chooses to be kind
Without conforming, is a magical being of this
earthly experience.
To be in love, to give grace despite the darkness
and callousness within,
To know oneself is the calling of life.
To strive toward love for oneself and for another,
The path of trauma forever shows the shadow
and the ego.
For the soul's essence to be poured onto the
wounds formed,
Shielding the light buried deep within,
Only for it to be awakened when the soul
engulfs the shadow,
Keeping the ego and the self's soul in the eternal
dance called life.
The process of shedding trauma through the
power of being in the now, in mind with a later,
The beauty of the universe shone through human
life.

Setting Fire

I had a dream of a yule knot,
Made with all wishes of the heart,
Tearing it all apart,
Making it into a poetic art.
Takes nothing but a part of my soul,
Forever burning the dream of bells.
For none that I have shared life with are worthy,
Nor dare to walk along these trails of life.

A gift of mercy shown by the self,
Showing all situations,
Seeing traditions turned into labels, put up on a
shelf,
For the world to see as decorations.

Of the vicarious experiences,
Never tied in bravery or truth,
Beautifully played in other obediences,
Burying the act of love, only to soothe
The emptiness of a self prone to meager
cravings,
Catching feelings, attaching false paintings.

As the truth of this world's reality hits,
A heavy toll takes on my spirits,
Making my heart eventually numb
To the false way forward,
Agreed upon by humans to thrive,
Creating a false self,
Completely defeated by the wants of love,
Setting all dreams on fire
Is the only way for my truth to thrive.

Belief

How do you define belief?
A mere thought? A desire?
A want? Or a need?
Believing is like magic,
A string of fate woven from destiny,
Completely unbiased about the physicality of
life.
A hope born out of the heart,
A charm of protection against intruders,
Of utter despair and discontent.

Made by thought, fueled by desire,
Birthing a series of paths of wants and needs.
What do you do when you do not believe
anymore?
Giving up is not a choice;
Staying stuck is not what is needed.
The passage of time teaches many things;
Of perseverance, of resilience,
Of love, of disappointments.

But the hardest thing is the acceptance of what it
is
When the belief had been so strongly rooted in
the soul.
To break a certain belief takes away your life,
Making me realize the saying "the walking
dead."
The difficulty of being in the flow,
To let go of resistance to what is not,
To move away for the sake of living.

A breath of fresh playfulness desperately
awaited.
It is not a circle that one goes around,
But the path of spirals,
Revisiting the need for a lost touch.
Looking back, what is the truth?
What was or what is?
Why does it all matter to the mind

When the heart cannot be in the now?

Praying for respite, the only way is through the
heart to God.
To take a step one by one,
to make do with the courage,
To face the unknown, to not pursue the answers
for a burnt life.
Take heart in the now; being water is difficult,
But it is the calmest and most powerful element
to be.

To move, to flow, to be,
To carve into the rocks of life,
To chip away at the harshness of conformity,
To let go of the person who is no more,
To create a self in a better way for now and later,
To have no regrets about the life that is burnt.
Such is belief, a magical essence of life.

Artist

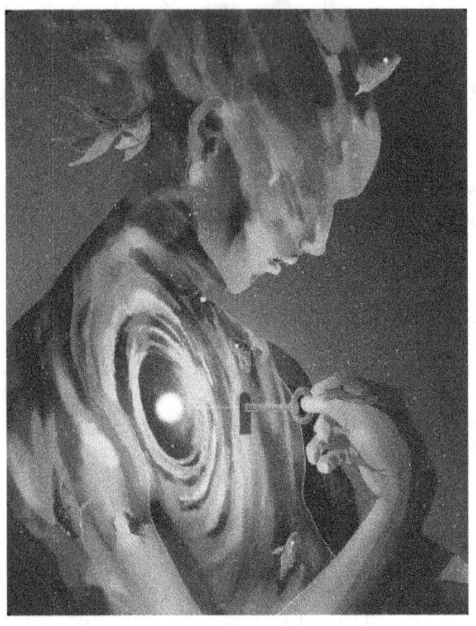

When one transforms into an artist,
Engulfing oneself in blue flames is a need,
Pushing the phoenix within to burn oneself
To be born anew.
When does one become an artist?
Or the better question: why does one become an
artist?
Is it to show the pain?
Or is it to tell a tale of what happened?
Or is it to pave the way to survive and thrive?
It is to break the construct of false realities to
seek truth.

The journey of an artist is to seek
Of the truth hiding among the meek.
To take the experiences,
To break the invariances,
To immerse thyself in grace,
Showing that there is no race
Of the living, of the being.
Love, a simple truth,
Severing all darkness with a sawtooth.
An artist is ever an enigma,
Having the alchemy to break the stigma.

See, the beauty of it all lies in the heart,
The one that feels the depth of its emotions,
turning it into art.
As for the mind, it is the door to a veil
Of how one chooses to put forth the past of pale,
Bearing the soul on a tremendous journey of
chaos,
Always offering oneself up to the spirits in a
loving séance.
All burdens and worries fall away in the process,
Showing the journey is not for the weak or the
depressed.

So listen, the truth of the art and its artist:
It is not the validation that is sought;
It is the tale of the truth shown,

A moment of awe for others,
Underlining the consciousness in wonders.
So the art is created in the hope of touching
another soul,
To say, not to worry, that this reality has been
existing.
For all humanity is to love, but it has chosen the
greed of perishables,
To give solace that another exists in authenticity,
Transmuting the energy of an artist from Chaos
to Order.

www.ingramcontent.com/pod-product-compliance
Lightning Source LLC
La Vergne TN
LVHW011042200726